Fantastic Kids

Malala Yousafzai

Dona Herweck Rice

Publishing Credits

Rachelle Cracchiolo, M.S.Ed., *Publisher*
Conni Medina, M.A.Ed., *Managing Editor*
Nika Fabienke, Ed.D., *Series Developer*
June Kikuchi, *Content Director*
Seth Rogers, *Editor*
Michelle Jovin, M.A., *Assistant Editor*
Lee Aucoin, *Senior Graphic Designer*

TIME For Kids and the TIME For Kids logo are registered trademarks of TIME Inc. Used under license.

Image Credits: Cover and p.1 Creative Commons Attribution 2.0 Generic by Simon Davis/United Kingdom Department for International Development; Reader's Page Andrew Burton/Getty Images; pp.4–5 White House Photo/Alamy Stock Photo; p.6 Photo by Christopher Furlong/Getty Images; pp.6–7, 24–25 Illustrations by Timothy J. Bradley; p.8 (inset) Mian Khursheed/For The Washington Post via Getty Images; pp.8–9 Metin Aktas/Anadolu Agency/Getty Images; pp.10–11 Tony Karumba/AFP/Getty Images; pp.14, 27 A. Majeed/AFP/Getty Images; p.15 Pakistan-Malala/Reuters/Faisal Mahmood Nuralya/Dreamstime.com; p.16 AFP/Tony Karumba/AFP/Getty Images; p.17 John Russo/Contour by Getty Images; pp.22–23 Naomi Goggin/Alamy Stock Photo; p.23 (bottom) Mark Pearson/Alamy Stock Photo; p.26 (bottom) Christopher Furlong/Getty Images; p.29 Veronique de Viguerie/Getty Images; pp.30–31 travelib asia/Alamy Stock Photo; p.31 PID/PAK IMAGES/Newscom; p.32 Rashid Mahmood/AFP/Getty Images; p.33 © Fox Searchlight PicturesEntertainment Pictures/ZUMAPRESS.com/Alamy Stock Photo; pp.34–35 Queen Elizabeth Hospital Birmingham via Getty Images; pp.36–37 Niu Xiaolei/Xinhua/Alamy Live News; p.37 (left) Pictorial Press Ltd/Alamy Stock Photo, (right) Reg Lancaster/Express/Getty Images; p.39 Mian Khursheed/Reuters; pp.40–41 (background) Maciej Dakowicz/Alamy Stock Photo; p.40 © Jamil Ahmed/Xinhua/Alamy Live News; p.41 KGC-42/starmaxinc.com/Newscom; p.48 Fox Searchlight Pictures/Entertainment Pictures/Alamy Stock Photo; all other images from iStock and/or Shutterstock.

All companies and products mentioned in this book are registered trademarks of their respective owners or developers and are used in this book strictly for editorial purposes; no commercial claim to their use is made by the author or the publisher.

Library of Congress Cataloging-in-Publication Data

Names: Rice, Dona, author.
Title: Malala Yousafzai / Dona Herweck Rice.
Description: Huntington Beach, CA : Teacher Created Materials, 2018. | Series: Fantastic kids | Includes index.
Identifiers: LCCN 2017023525 (print) | LCCN 2017024610 (ebook) | ISBN 9781425854645 (eBook) | ISBN 9781425849887 (pbk.)
Subjects: LCSH: Yousafzai, Malala, 1997---Juvenile literature. | Girls--Education--Pakistan--Juvenile literature. | Girls--Violence against--Pakistan--Juvenile literature. | Women social reformers--Pakistan--Biography--Juvenile literature. | Taliban--Juvenile literature. | Pakistan--Social conditions--Juvenile literature.
Classification: LCC LC2330 (ebook) | LCC LC2330 .R53 2018 (print) | DDC 371.822095491--dc23
LC record available at https://lccn.loc.gov/2017023525

Teacher Created Materials

5301 Oceanus Drive
Huntington Beach, CA 92649-1030
http://www.tcmpub.com

ISBN 978-1-4258-4988-7

© 2018 Teacher Created Materials, Inc.
Printed in China

Table of Contents

Do the Right Thing

How far would you go to defend what you believe is right? Would you stand up to bullies? Would you speak for the **oppressed**? Would you still do so even if you had to sacrifice your own comfort? *Would you risk your life?*

Every person is challenged at some point to do what is right, but not everyone is called to risk personal safety for the greater good. Doing the right thing takes courage no matter the situation; doing the right thing when your life is at risk is an **exceptional** act of bravery.

Malala Yousafzai (mah-LAH-lah yoo-sahf-ZAY) demonstrated such bravery as a child—and nearly lost her life. But the positive **impact** she had is still **reverberating** around the world.

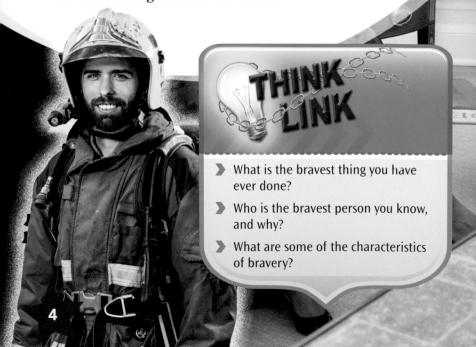

THINK LINK

> What is the bravest thing you have ever done?

> Who is the bravest person you know, and why?

> What are some of the characteristics of bravery?

Malala Yousafzai meets with President Barack Obama at the White House.

Now a Woman

Malala was born in 1997 and is now an adult. The actions that make her extraordinary began when she was just a young girl.

Just a Girl

On July 12, 1997, a little girl was born to Toor Pekai (TORE peh-KAY) and Ziauddin (zee-ow-DEEN) Yousafzai. The baby—who they named Malala—was born at home in the Swat Valley in a city named Mingora in the country of Pakistan.

Like many people there, Malala and her family lived in **poverty**. But they were happy. Her home was filled with love. Her parents had jobs that satisfied them. The landscape around her home was beautiful. There was a warm **culture** of food, art, and music. The girl was born into this welcoming family.

From left to right: Malala's father, her brothers, her mother, and Malala

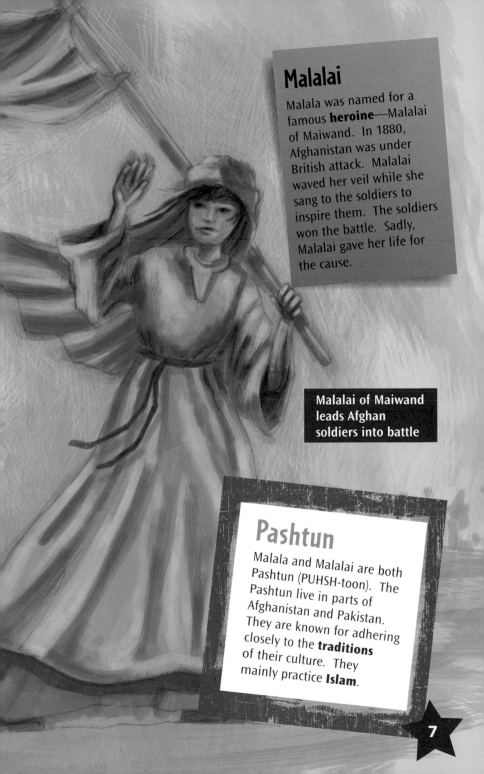

Malalai

Malala was named for a famous **heroine**—Malalai of Maiwand. In 1880, Afghanistan was under British attack. Malalai waved her veil while she sang to the soldiers to inspire them. The soldiers won the battle. Sadly, Malalai gave her life for the cause.

Malalai of Maiwand leads Afghan soldiers into battle

Pashtun

Malala and Malalai are both Pashtun (PUHSH-toon). The Pashtun live in parts of Afghanistan and Pakistan. They are known for adhering closely to the **traditions** of their culture. They mainly practice **Islam**.

7

As welcoming as Malala's world was, there was a marked difference between her life and a boy's life. When a baby boy is born, the people in her community offer congratulations, food, and gifts. They do not do these things for a baby girl. When Malala's two younger brothers were born, the neighborhood celebrated. They did not celebrate Malala's birth.

This was the culture that Malala was born into. Boys would one day grow up to be leaders of their families. Girls would grow up to support men.

A Pleasant Place

Mingora is known for its summer festivals. When Malala was young, many tourists came to enjoy the music in her town. During the winter, people went there for skiing vacations.

A local man pushes a cart into Mingora.

The Gift of Children

Malala's grandfather—her father's father—was a **devout** Muslim. He taught his son, Ziauddin, that all children—boys and girls—are sacred gifts from Allah, or God. He thought that all children should be cared for, taught, and respected.

Something More

From the time she was little, Malala had a vision for something more for her life. Her parents saw **value** in all children, boys and girls. Malala saw this as well, and she believed she could make her dreams come true.

Malala loved to learn, and she studied and read everything she could. She liked to play school, pretending that she was the teacher. Malala was determined to make something of her life and to support others while doing it. She decided she wanted to become a doctor.

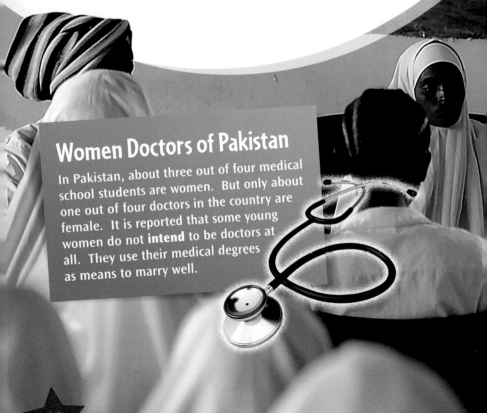

Women Doctors of Pakistan

In Pakistan, about three out of four medical school students are women. But only about one out of four doctors in the country are female. It is reported that some young women do not **intend** to be doctors at all. They use their medical degrees as means to marry well.

Married Young

Women in Pakistan get married when they are young. The average age is 21 years old. In the United States, the average age is older. American women typically get married when they are 27 years old.

Malala giving a speech to women in Kenya.

Education

There are 32 million girls around the world who will not receive an eighth-grade-level education. There are 98 million more girls who will not receive a high school education. That is a total of 130 million girls! The right to an education affects many areas of a woman's life. Here are a few ways in which girls with at least an eighth-grade-level education find it easier to succeed.

The death rate for women giving birth would be reduced, which would save 98,000 lives a year. This is mainly because educated mothers are more likely to have their babies in hospitals, where doctors are available to help in emergencies.

The annual death rate for children would drop by nearly 1 million. If all mothers finished high school, the death rate for children would be cut in half, saving 3 million lives a year.

The difference in pay between a man and a woman drops with equal education.

Comparing Wages of Men and Women by Country

Percent of Wages

	Canada	UK	U.S.	China	France
	62%	66%	64%	65%	50%

Educated mothers are twice as likely to send their children to school, creating a cycle of educated women.

Nearly 2 million children would be saved from **stunting** caused by hunger each year. If those mothers also finished high school, that number jumps to 12 million.

School Days

Malala's mother, Toor Pekai, attended school for a short time and loved it. However, it was not common during her childhood for girls to go to school. Although she did not continue her education, her dream of learning did not leave her.

Malala's father, Ziauddin, on the other hand, stayed in school. His father had been a teacher, and Ziauddin knew that school was an **invaluable resource** to him while he was growing up. He believed that school taught him to think for himself. Ziauddin grew up to become a teacher, too. In fact, he opened his own school, and Malala was one of his students.

Why a School for Girls?

One of the reasons Ziauddin started a school for girls was because his five sisters had to stay home when he went to school as a boy. Ziauddin didn't think this was fair. It became a passion for him to educate all children.

High Marks

Ziauddin opened and ran a school in Mingora. The Khushal Girls High School is for girls only. Malala was considered a top student at Khushal.

a student of
Khushal Girls
High School, 2013

15

Malala enjoyed school, and she wanted to be there as often as she could. Her friends were there, of course, but Malala truly loved learning. She read, wrote, and studied with a **voracious** appetite!

Malala also learned at home. She learned household work from her mother and neighboring women. This work was highly valued. But she mainly enjoyed listening to the men who gathered with her father to discuss politics and the world. From them, she learned a great deal about how the world is run. She became determined to make a difference in the world herself.

Malala and Ziauddin speak about the importance of education.

Three Languages

Malala studied and mastered three languages while at her father's school. She studied Urdu, which is the official language of her country. Malala also learned English and Pashto. Pashto is the everyday language of her people.

A Bigger Dream

Ziauddin wanted all of the children of Pakistan to get an education. But his dream became realized in a bigger way than he imagined. Now, he works at the United Nations (UN). He is the special advisor for global education. His dreams for education now impact the world!

Student of Culture

One thing that made Malala aware of the world as a whole was her knowledge of culture. Her own culture was rich, and she enjoyed it. Her father often shared traditional writings. One of his favorites was the work of Jalāl al-Dīn Rūmī (juh-LAL ahl-DEEN ROO-me), a poet from long ago.

Malala and her family also enjoyed learning about cultures from around the world. They listened to **Western** music. (Malala liked Justin Bieber.) They watched Western shows. (Malala's favorite was *Ugly Betty*.) They read Western books. (Malala loved the Twilight series.) Many tourists came to the Swat Valley and shared their cultures. All of these people made Malala sensitive to cultures other than her own. She valued hers but appreciated others, too.

In a Spin

Rūmī wrote thousands of poems. Often, he thought of his poems while twirling in a **meditative** style. He spoke his poems and someone else wrote them down as he twirled. Many people consider his poetry to be spiritually based.

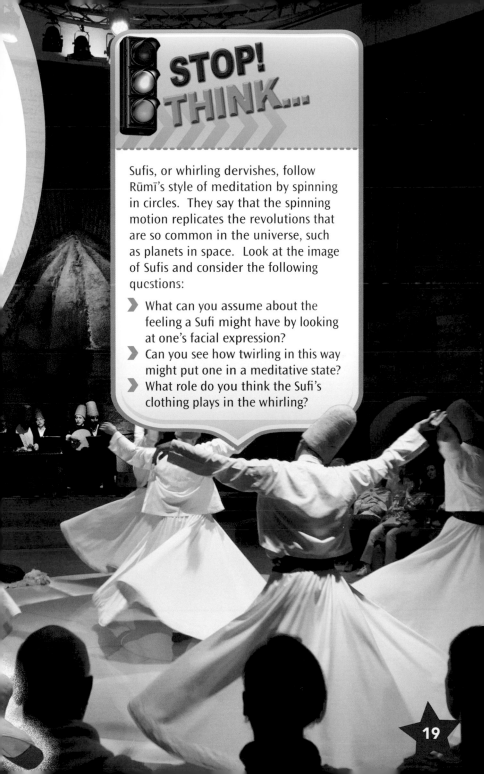

Sufis, or whirling dervishes, follow Rūmī's style of meditation by spinning in circles. They say that the spinning motion replicates the revolutions that are so common in the universe, such as planets in space. Look at the image of Sufis and consider the following questions:

> What can you assume about the feeling a Sufi might have by looking at one's facial expression?
> Can you see how twirling in this way might put one in a meditative state?
> What role do you think the Sufi's clothing plays in the whirling?

War in the Valley

When Malala was about 10 years old, her world changed completely. A strict and violent group called the Taliban came to power in Afghanistan. Its members have very extreme ideas. Under the Taliban, women are powerless. Girls cannot go to school. Women cannot work or vote. Male relatives must **escort** women and girls in public. Women must also be covered from head to toe.

The Taliban began to invade Malala's country, and word spread that all girls would be kept from school. Malala was shocked. School was everything to her. She felt that everyone had a right to an education! How could such a terrible thing happen?

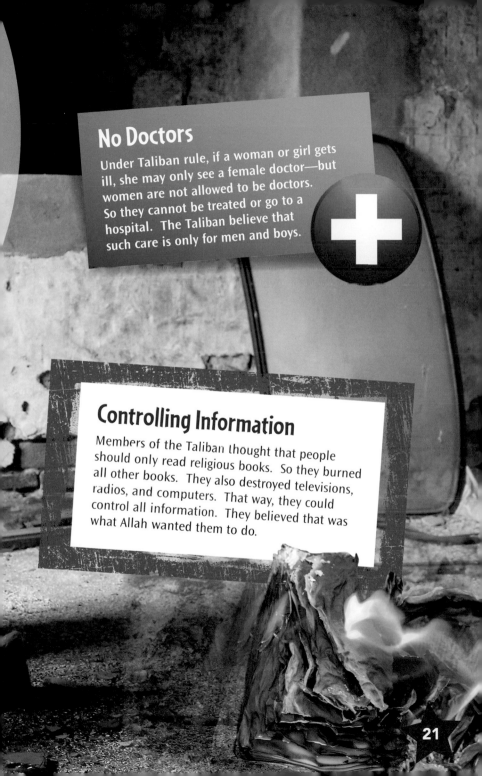

No Doctors

Under Taliban rule, if a woman or girl gets ill, she may only see a female doctor—but women are not allowed to be doctors. So they cannot be treated or go to a hospital. The Taliban believe that such care is only for men and boys.

Controlling Information

Members of the Taliban thought that people should only read religious books. So they burned all other books. They also destroyed televisions, radios, and computers. That way, they could control all information. They believed that was what Allah wanted them to do.

Taliban leaders told Ziauddin to close his school. Many schools were being destroyed, as were public places that involved music and dance. **Armed** Taliban soldiers seemed to be everywhere. They invaded homes and businesses. They ruled the streets. People fled to find safety and freedom elsewhere.

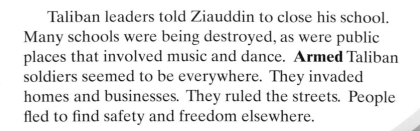

Peace and Fellowship

Members of the Taliban say that they practice Islam, but their form of Islam is not what other Muslims around the world practice. Islam embraces peace, fellowship, and care for one's neighbors. The Taliban does not.

The Taliban burned this building in the Swat Valley.

The Pakistan Army arrived to fight the Taliban, and the two groups were at war for more than a year. The army was able to push back the Taliban—but the Taliban did not go away. People were still being threatened, beaten, or killed. Despite the risk, some children bravely went to school, including Malala. But no one was safe.

Gone

When the war was over, more than half of the people in the Swat Valley had fled. More than 150 schools for girls in Mingora had been destroyed.

A girl carries all her belongings as she leaves the Swat Valley.

DIG DEEPER

Under Cover

Muslim women are expected to dress **modestly**. Modesty can mean different things to different people. Many women wear some kind of veil to cover part, if not all, of their heads and bodies. Malala wears a covering called a *hijab*.

The Taliban insists on women being fully covered. They say it is for their religion. Some people believe that it is really to **subjugate** women.

Here are some of the coverings Muslim women wear:

**hijab
(hih-JAHB)**

a veil that covers the head, hair, and neck, but not the face

**dupatta
(doo-PAHT-tah)**

a long, flowing scarf that is worn around the head, neck, and shoulders

**chador
(CHAH-dohr)**

a large piece of cloth that is wrapped around the head and upper body leaving only the face exposed

Rules of Grooming

A *hadith*, or saying that is credited to Muhammad, is that men should grow their beards but trim their mustaches. Under the Taliban in Pakistan, men had to grow their beards under threat of punishment.

niqab
(nih-KAHB)

a head veil covering all but the eyes; often worn with an abaya, a long, loose covering for the body

burqa
(BUHR-kah)

a veil that fully covers a woman's head, face, and body, with mesh across the eyes

Malala Speaks

In late 2008, the Taliban warned that only boys could return to school after the winter break. The British Broadcasting Corporation (BBC) kept a website that was written in Urdu. A reporter for the BBC wanted someone in Pakistan to speak out about the schools closing. Ziauddin had always been outspoken about education for all. The reporter turned to him for help.

Ziauddin could not get one of his teachers to speak. They were too afraid. But he had an idea. Malala had strong opinions and a brave heart. She could write under a **pseudonym**. In this way, she could stay safe. Malala agreed to do it. She was just 11 years old.

Protecting Her Father

Even with a fake name, Malala was worried about writing for the BBC. She was afraid the Taliban would **retaliate** against her father. She was not worried for herself. Her father was not worried either. He did not think the Taliban would come after a child.

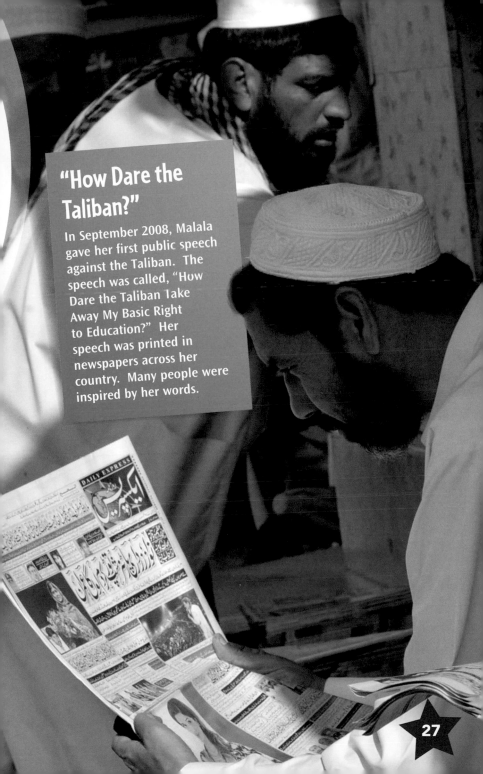

"How Dare the Taliban?"

In September 2008, Malala gave her first public speech against the Taliban. The speech was called, "How Dare the Taliban Take Away My Basic Right to Education?" Her speech was printed in newspapers across her country. Many people were inspired by her words.

A Schoolgirl's Diary

Malala started a **blog** for the BBC in early 2009 titled "Diary of a Pakistani Schoolgirl." She wrote under the name *Gul Makai*. She wrote down her thoughts and read her notes to a reporter. The reporter then posted her blog.

Celebrity Status

At the same time Malala was writing her blog, *The New York Times* began filming a movie about the Taliban. Malala and Ziauddin are shown in the film. Because of her father's work, Malala was also interviewed on a talk show in Pakistan. She was asked how she felt about the closing of schools.

Most of her country wanted education for girls. In February, the Taliban let girls go back to school. But there was still fighting, and the streets were unsafe. Many people fled the country, including the Yousafzai family. They returned in July when the Taliban was forced out. But Malala was not safe. She had done some television interviews about her blog. The Taliban now knew who she was.

Malala and the computer she used to write her blog, in 2009

Gul Makai

Malala got her pseudonym from the heroine of a Pashtun folktale. She chose the name because it would have a deep meaning in her community. Malala thought the name would help people identify with her.

Back to School

Malala returned to school in August 2009 with a new dream. She now wanted to be a politician, not a doctor. Malala studied hard and continued to speak out "so that those without a voice can be heard."

For the next three years, Mingora slowly returned to what it had once been. Movie theaters opened again. Television shows returned. Once again, people filled the streets. Boys and girls returned to school. By October 2012, Malala was feeling excited for her future and eager to speak on causes she cared about.

Then, her whole world changed with a single shot.

National Youth Peace Prize

Pakistan's Prime Minister created a new award in 2011. It is given to the youth in Pakistan who has done the most for peace in the world. Malala won the first award (shown at right). After that, the name of the prize was changed to the National Malala Peace Prize.

And the Winner Is...

In 2011, Malala was nominated for The International Children's Peace Prize. This award is given to a child whose bravery makes a difference in the world. Malala did not win that year. But, she was nominated again in 2013. That time, she won.

GOVERNMENT OF PAKISTAN
NATIONAL YOUTH PEACE PRIZE
2011
MALALA YOUSAFZAI

A Defining Moment

On October 9, 2012, Malala and several classmates and teachers were riding on a school bus. The bus suddenly came to a stop, and a man appeared at the back with a gun. He raised his gun and shot Malala.

Police officers inspect the school bus where Malala was shot.

"Who Is Malala?"

When the Taliban soldier boarded the bus, he asked, "Who is Malala?" No one answered him. Some girls thought it might have been a reporter and quickly glanced in Malala's direction. The soldier then knew which girl was Malala.

Malala has no memory of the next week. She was rushed to one hospital and then another. She had a life-saving surgery. Finally, she was flown to a hospital in England.

On October 16, she awoke, but she could not speak and did not know where she was. Using a letter board, Malala spelled out two words to help gain understanding. The words were *country* and *father*.

Malala's Mother

Toor Pekai left school when she was six years old, so she never learned to read or write. On the day Malala was shot, she was scheduled to begin classes. She has since become **literate**.

Soon after Malala woke up, her family arrived in England. They lived in an apartment so they could be near her. Malala had to remain in the hospital for months. Her breathing tube was eventually removed, and she could speak again. She had been shot in the head and neck. The doctors said it was amazing that she lived. Malala had damage to her facial muscles and hearing.

The path to recovery would take many months— but Malala *would* recover. Despite the terrible attack, the Taliban had not stopped her. Malala still had her voice. Now, she had a new **resolve** to speak.

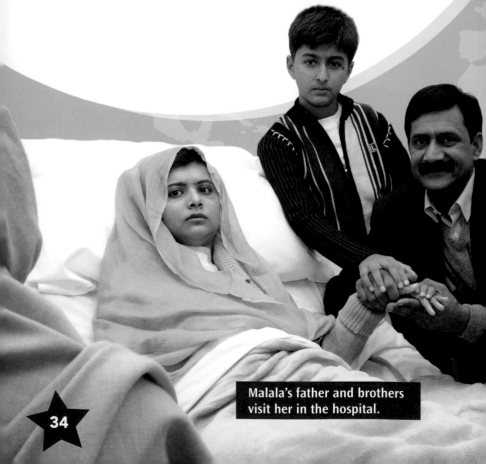

Malala's father and brothers visit her in the hospital.

England

"Visiting" Home

While in England, the whole family missed their home in Pakistan. But they wanted the best care for Malala, and Pakistan was not safe for any of them. Malala used Skype™ to visit with friends back home.

Pakistan

Other Victims

Two other girls on the bus were shot at the same time as Malala. Their injuries were not life threatening, and they, too, survived.

Honored

After the shooting, Malala became a worldwide celebrity. Members of the United Nations **designated** her 16th birthday as Malala Day and asked her to speak at its New York headquarters. Her recovery was going well, so she made the trip. In her passionate speech, Malala declared, "I speak not for myself, but for those without a voice [so they] can be heard. Those who have fought for their rights. Their right to live in peace. Their right to be treated with dignity. Their right to equality of opportunity. Their right to be educated."

Unhappy at Home

Many people in Pakistan respect Malala. But not everyone does. Some people live in fear. They fear retaliation each time Malala speaks.

A New Hero

Malala's heroes are people who risk their lives to stand up for what they know is right. Mahatma Gandhi (left), Mother Teresa (center), and Martin Luther King Jr. (right) rank near the top of her list. Now, many people add Malala to their own lists.

Malala had not been silenced. In fact, her voice and message were now stronger. She said, "Education is the only solution." People around the world heard her and cheered for her.

Malala was so popular that she was asked to write a book. *I Am Malala* was published not long after her UN talk. A children's version of the book came out the next year.

Nobel Peace Prize

When he died, Swedish scientist Alfred Nobel left funds to be given as a prize. Each year, the award honors someone who played a big role in one of six lines of work. Many of Malala's heroes, such as Nelson Mandela and King, won the Nobel Peace Prize, too.

display at the Nobel Peace Center in Norway

Malala's highest honor came in late 2014. She was named co-winner of the Nobel Peace Prize. The award honored her fight "for the right of all children to education." She was the youngest person ever to receive the award.

Paying It Forward

The Nobel Prize comes with a large cash award. Malala used her money for the Malala Fund, which builds and repairs schools around the world.

A woman reads *I Am Malala* in a bookstore in Pakistan.

Learning for All

Many children do not realize that in some places, kids are not given the chance to learn. Going to school is still strictly forbidden for some children—mainly girls—around the world.

Malala has dedicated her life to **ensure** that all children have a chance to go to school. She knows the difference that learning can make in a person's life. She knows, too, the difference it can make in a community.

Malala thinks of education as a human right. She knows that there are many troubles in the world. But, as she says, "Education is the only solution."

He Named Me Malala

Malala has released a documentary movie about her life and experiences. It is called *He Named Me Malala*. The "he" of the title is her father.

Feminists and Friends

Malala now refers to herself as a **feminist**. She was inspired to claim the label after hearing actress Emma Watson speak on the subject. The two women have since become friends.

Glossary

armed—carrying weapons

blog—a website on which a person or people write about opinions, activities, or experiences

culture—the beliefs and ways of a group of people

designated—to officially give something a particular role or purpose

devout—deeply religious

ensure—to make sure of something

escort—to serve as a companion

exceptional—uncommon or unusual

feminist—a person who believes that men and women should have equal rights and opportunities

heroine—a woman who is admired for her brave acts or great characteristics

impact—effect or outcome

intend—to want or plan to do something

invaluable—extremely valuable

Islam—the religion of Muslims

literate—able to read and write

meditative—involving deep thought

modestly—to dress in a way that covers most of the body

oppressed—a person or group of people treated in a cruel or unfair way

poverty—the state of having little or no money

pseudonym—fake name used in place of a real name

resolve—determination

resource—a thing that provides something useful and necessary

retaliate—to do something bad to get back at someone

reverberating—echoing with sound

stunting—stopping someone from growing or developing

subjugate—to defeat and make obedient

traditions—ways of thinking or doing things that have been done by a particular group of people for a long time

value—worth

voracious—having an inclination to eat or take in a great deal

Western—of or relating to countries in North America and Western Europe

Index

Check It Out!

Books

Abouraya, Karen Leggett. 2014. *Malala Yousafzai: Warrior with Words*. Starwalk Kids Media.

Brown, Dinah. 2015. *Who Is Malala Yousafzai?*. Grosset and Dunlap.

Ellis, Deborah. 2015. *Mud City*. Groundwood Books.

Staples, Suzanne Fisher. 2008. *Under the Persimmon Tree*. Square Fish.

Yousafzai, Malala and Patricia McCormick. 2015. *I Am Malala: How One Girl Stood Up for Education and Changed the World* (Young Readers Edition). Little, Brown Books for Young Readers.

Websites

BBC News. *Diary of a Pakistani schoolgirl*. http://news.bbc.co.uk/2/hi/south_asia/7834402.stm

Malala Fund. www.malala.org

United Nations. www.un.org

Video

Guggenheim, Davis. *He Named Me Malala*. Fox Searchlight Pictures and National Geographic, 2015.

Yousafzai, Ziauddin. *My Daughter, Malala*. TED, 2014.

Try It!

Malala almost gave up her life for her passionate belief that all children deserve a chance to receive an education. What is something in your life that you are passionate about?

❯ Choose a topic. Some ideas may include education, the environment, sports, or art.

❯ Write a paragraph about how your cause can be improved. Does your soccer team need new uniforms? Does your school band need new instruments?

❯ Share your opinion paper with friends and family members, and ask them to help your cause.

❯ If you still need more help, send your letter to a local politician, and ask for help.

About the Author

Dona Herweck Rice has a few personal heroes, including some of Malala's—such as Dr. King and Gandhi. She admires people who take a stand for justice and fairness and speak up for the downtrodden. She respects those who fight (peacefully!) for equality for all. She also values those who use the power of words to change the world for good. Rice considers the ability to use words well a real-life superpower! Malala certainly has that gift. Now Malala is one of Rice's personal heroes, too. Rice is the author of hundreds of books on a variety of topics for children of all ages. She lives in Southern California with her husband and two sons.